I0408835

About the National Science and Technology Council

The National Science and Technology Council (NSTC) is the principal means by which the Executive Branch coordinates science and technology policy across the diverse entities that make up the Federal research and development (R&D) enterprise. One of the NSTC's primary objectives is establishing clear national goals for Federal science and technology investments. The NSTC prepares R&D packages aimed at accomplishing multiple national goals. The NSTC's work is organized under five committees: Environment, Natural Resources, and Sustainability; Homeland and National Security; Science, Technology, Engineering, and Mathematics (STEM) Education; Science; and Technology. Each of these committees oversees subcommittees and working groups that are focused on different aspects of science and technology. More information is available at www.whitehouse.gov/ostp/nstc.

About the Office of Science and Technology Policy

The Office of Science and Technology Policy (OSTP) was established by the National Science and Technology Policy, Organization, and Priorities Act of 1976. OSTP's responsibilities include advising the President in policy formulation and budget development on questions in which science and technology are important elements; articulating the President's science and technology policy and programs; and fostering strong partnerships among Federal, state, and local governments, and the scientific communities in industry and academia. The Director of OSTP also serves as Assistant to the President for Science and Technology and manages the NSTC. More information is available at www.whitehouse.gov/ostp.

About the Subcommittee on Networking and Information Technology Research and Development

The Subcommittee on Networking and Information Technology Research and Development (NITRD), also known as the NITRD Program, is a body under the Committee on Technology (CoT) of the NSTC. The NITRD Subcommittee coordinates multiagency research and development programs to help assure continued U.S. leadership in networking and information technology, satisfy the needs of the Federal Government for advanced networking and information technology, and accelerate development and deployment of advanced networking and information technology. It also implements relevant provisions of the High-Performance Computing Act of 1991 (P.L. 102-194), as amended by the Next Generation Internet Research Act of 1998 (P.L. 105-305), and the America Creating Opportunities to Meaningfully Promote Excellence in Technology, Education and Science (COMPETES) Act of 2007 (P.L. 110-69). For more information, see www.nitrd.gov.

Copyright Information

June 24, 2016

Dear Colleagues:

Advances in networking and information technologies are among key elements for U.S. economic growth and are essential to progress in many domains. Underpinning this progress are often large-scale collection, processing, and archiving of information. However, the vast increase in the quantity of personal information that is being collected and retained, combined with the increased ability to analyze it and fuse it with other information, is creating valid concerns about privacy. Given these concerns, the Federal Government supports the need to increase research and development in privacy-enhancing technologies and related science.

We are pleased to transmit with this letter the National Science and Technology Council's (NSTC) *National Privacy Research Strategy* (NPRS), developed by the Networking and Information Technology Research and Development (NITRD) Program. It was developed in light of the government's recognition of the challenges to personal privacy from large-scale deployment of information technology systems and from the challenges presented by "Big Data." The strategy responds to the 2014 reports, *Big Data: Seizing Opportunities, Preserving Values* by the White House and *Big Data and Privacy: A Technological Perspective* by the President's Council of Advisors on Science and Technology (PCAST).

This strategy establishes objectives and priorities for Federally-funded privacy research, provides a framework for coordinating privacy research and development, and encourages multi-disciplinary research that recognizes privacy needs of individuals and society and the responsibilities of the government. The science and technology advances established by this strategy will enable individuals, commercial entities, and the government to benefit from technological advancements and provide meaningful protections for personal information and individual privacy.

We are pleased to commend this *National Privacy Research Strategy* as part of the Administration's comprehensive effort to protect fundamental values such as privacy and fairness, while advancing innovative information technologies. We look forward to working with Federal agencies, the private sector, and the public to realize that goal.

Sincerely,

James F. Kurose
Assistant Director, Computer and Information
Science and Engineering Directorate, National
Science Foundation

Keith A Marzullo
Director, National Coordination Office for
Networking and Information Technology
Research and Development

Co-Chairs, Subcommittee on Networking and Information Technology Research and Development

National Science and Technology Council

Chair
John P. Holdren
Assistant to the President for Science and Technology and Director, Office of Science and Technology Policy

Staff
Afua Bruce
Executive Director
Office of Science and Technology Policy

Subcommittee on Networking and Information Technology Research and Development

Co-Chair
James Kurose
Assistant Director, Computer and Information Science and Engineering Directorate
National Science Foundation

Co-Chair
Keith Marzullo
Director, National Coordination Office for Networking and Information Technology Research and Development

National Privacy Research Strategy Working Group

Marjory Blumenthal, Office of Science and Technology Policy

Sean Brooks, National Institute of Standards and Technology

Chris Clifton, National Science Foundation

Milton Corn, National Institutes of Health

Lorrie Cranor, Federal Trade Commission

Ed Doray, Department of Defense

Simson Garfinkel, National Institute of Standards and Technology

Marc Groman, Office of Management and Budget

Karyn Higa-Smith, Department of Homeland Security

Christa Jones, Census Bureau

Anthony Kelly, National Science Foundation

Erin Kenneally, Department of Homeland Security

Eva Kleederman, Office of the Director of National Intelligence

Carl Landwehr, National Security Agency

John Launchbury, Defense Advanced Research Projects Agency

Naomi Lefkovitz, National Institute of Standards and Technology

Jessica Lyon, Federal Trade Commission

David Marcos, National Security Agency

Keith Marzullo, National Coordination Office for NITRD

Gregg Motta, Federal Bureau of Investigation

Tristan Nguyen, Air Force Office of Scientific Research

Eugene Sullivan, National Security Agency

Tomas Vagoun, National Coordination Office for NITRD

Ralph Wachter, National Science Foundation

Heng Xu, National Science Foundation

Staff
Tomas Vagoun
National Coordination Office for Networking and Information Technology Research and Development

Table of Contents

1. Summary

People's lives are inextricably interconnected with cyberspace and information systems. The computing revolution is enabling advances in many sectors of the economy, while social interactions have been profoundly affected by the rise of the Internet and mobile communications. Increasing computerization and data collection in transportation, education, health care, and other areas will accelerate these trends. Massive data collection, processing, and retention in the digital era challenge long-established privacy norms. On the one hand, large-scale data analytics is indispensable to progress in science, engineering, and medicine; on the other hand, when information about individuals and their activities can be tracked and repurposed without the individual's knowledge or understanding, opportunities emerge for unauthorized disclosure, embarrassment and harassment, social stigma, crime, discrimination, and misuse. The fact that such an opportunity exists can itself have a detrimental and chilling effect on people's behaviors.

The Federal Government is mindful of this risk, and the resulting need for research and development. The White House report *Big Data: Seizing Opportunities, Preserving Values*[1] highlights the need for large-scale privacy research: "We should dramatically increase investment for research and development in privacy-enhancing technologies, encouraging cross-cutting research that involves not only computer science and mathematics, but also social science, communications, and legal disciplines."

The National Privacy Research Strategy establishes objectives for Federally-funded privacy research (both extramural and government-internal research), provides a structure for coordinating research and development in privacy-enhancing technologies, and encourages multi-disciplinary research that recognizes the responsibilities of the government and the needs of society. The overarching goal of this strategy is to produce knowledge and technology that will enable individuals, commercial entities, and the government to benefit from transformative technological advancements, enhance opportunities for innovation, and provide meaningful protections for personal information and individual privacy.

To achieve these goals, this strategy identifies the following priorities for privacy research:

- Foster multidisciplinary approach to privacy research and solutions;
- Understand and measure privacy desires and impacts;
- Develop system design methods that incorporate privacy desires, requirements, and controls;
- Increase transparency of data collection, sharing, use, and retention;
- Assure that information flows and use are consistent with privacy rules;
- Develop approaches for remediation and recovery; and
- Reduce privacy risks of analytical algorithms.

---

[1] "Big Data: Seizing Opportunities, Preserving Values," The White House, May 2014, http://www.whitehouse.gov/sites/default/files/docs/big_data_privacy_report_may_1_2014.pdf.

2. Introduction

2.1 Privacy Research Purpose

Networking and information technology is transforming life in the 21st century, changing the way people, businesses, and government interact. Vast improvements in computing, storage, and communications are creating new opportunities for enhancing our social wellbeing; improving health and health care; eliminating barriers to education and employment; and increasing efficiencies in many sectors such as manufacturing, transportation, and agriculture.

The promise of these new applications often stems from their ability to create, collect, transmit, process, and archive information on a massive scale. However, the vast increase in the quantity of personal information that is being collected and retained, combined with the increased ability to analyze it and combine it with other information, is creating valid concerns about privacy and about the ability of entities to manage these unprecedented volumes of data responsibly. When information about people and their activities can be collected, analyzed, tracked, and repurposed in so many ways, it can lead to crime, discrimination, unauthorized and inadvertent disclosure, embarrassment and harassment, social stigma, inappropriate decisions, and other outcomes that may disadvantage them. That such possibilities exist can create a chilling effect on people's behaviors, which can be a significant harm in itself. A key challenge of this era is to assure that growing capabilities to create, capture, store, and process vast quantities of information will not damage the core values of the country.

For more than a century, citizens, lawmakers, and academics have been concerned about the effect of new technologies on personal privacy. For almost as long, U.S. legislation has provided specific privacy protections to consumers in an expanding set of areas. However, the progress of privacy understanding and protection has not kept pace with the exponential increase in data collection, processing, and storage, and the resulting risks to privacy. Today, information exists in a complex and dynamic ecosystem that includes the collectors, who may or may not have a relationship with the individual; data brokers, who buy, repackage, and sell collected information; analytics providers, who create systems for processing such information; and data users, who make decisions based upon the analytics. The plummeting cost of storage has allowed organizations to collect large amounts of data and save the data in long-term repositories, making such data available for unanticipated future use. Meanwhile, there is a growing array of always-on consumer devices, environmental sensors, and tracking technologies designed to collect, process, and archive information continuously, often without the individual knowing exactly what is being collected about him or her and how it will be used.

It is these substantial increases in the type and amount of data collected, the scale of the analysis, and the uncertainty of their use that is driving the current increase in privacy concerns. The availability of disparate datasets is setting the stage for a "mosaic effect,"[2] where analysis across data sets can reveal

---

[2] "Open Data Policy-Managing Information as an Asset," White House Office of Management and Budget, May 9, 2013, https://www.whitehouse.gov/sites/default/files/omb/memoranda/2013/m-13-13.pdf.

private information or generate inaccurate inferences, even though in isolation the data sets may not raise privacy issues.

In response to this technological progress, this Administration has taken an active role in providing leadership across a broad range of privacy issues. In the area of protecting online privacy, the Administration released in 2011 the *National Strategy for Trusted Identities in Cyberspace*,[3] providing a roadmap for the public and private sectors to collaborate in increasing privacy and trust in online identities. In the area of consumer privacy, the Administration released in 2012 a careful analysis of consumer privacy issues and set out the "Consumer Privacy Bill of Rights," which provides a set of principles that consumers should be able to expect from products and services.[4] Most recently, the release of *Big Data: A Report on Algorithmic Systems, Opportunity, and Civil Rights*[5] continues the Administration's examination of the potential privacy and discrimination risks that exist in deploying big data and algorithmic systems.

In 2014, the U.S. Government's investment in Networking and Information Technology Research and Development was $3.9 billion.[6] Within that total, the investment in privacy research activities was approximately $80 million.[7] These research investments include explicit privacy efforts in health care, privacy regulation compliance, and multidisciplinary privacy research explorations, as well as research on privacy as an extension of other research on computer security. Although important, this work has not been coordinated with an overall strategy and desired goals, and as a result it has not met its full potential.

---

[3] "National Strategy for Trusted Identities in Cyberspace: Enhancing Online Choice, Efficiency, Security, and Privacy," The White House, April 2011, https://www.whitehouse.gov/sites/default/files/rss_viewer/NSTICstrategy_041511.pdf.

[4] "Consumer Data Privacy in a Networked World: A Framework for Protecting Privacy and Promoting Innovation in the Global Digital Economy," The White House, February 2012, https://www.whitehouse.gov/sites/default/files/privacy-final.pdf. Following the release of the 2012 Consumer Data Privacy document, the Administration developed and released a discussion draft of a legislative proposal to translate the principles into legislation. "Administration Discussion Draft: Consumer Privacy Bill of Rights Act," The White House, February 2015, https://www.whitehouse.gov/sites/default/files/omb/legislative/letters/cpbr-act-of-2015-discussion-draft.pdf.

[5] "Big Data: A Report on Algorithmic Systems, Opportunity, and Civil Rights," The White House, May 2016, https://www.whitehouse.gov/sites/default/files/microsites/ostp/2016_0504_data_discrimination.pdf.

[6] "The Networking and Information Technology Research and Development Program, Supplement to the President's Budget, FY 2016," National Coordination Office for NITRD, February 2015, https://www.whitehouse.gov/sites/default/files/microsites/ostp/fy2016nitrdsupplement-final.pdf.

[7] "Report on Privacy Research within NITRD," National Coordination Office for NITRD, April 2014, https://www.nitrd.gov/Pubs/Report_on_Privacy_Research_within_NITRD.pdf.

The President's Council of Advisors on Science and Technology (PCAST) report[8] on big data and privacy calls for coordinating this research and using that coordination as impetus for increased Federal investments:

With coordination and encouragement from OSTP,[9] the NITRD agencies should strengthen U.S. research in privacy-related technologies and in the relevant areas of social science that inform the successful application of those technologies. Some of the technology for controlling uses already exists. However, research (and funding for it) is needed in the technologies that help to protect privacy, in the social mechanisms that influence privacy-preserving behavior, and in the legal options that are robust to changes in technology and create appropriate balance among economic opportunity, national priorities, and privacy protection.

In response to PCAST's recommendation, the National Privacy Research Strategy (NPRS) establishes strategic objectives for Federally-funded research in privacy and provides guidance to Federal agencies for developing and sponsoring research and development (R&D) activities in this area. This research aims to produce new knowledge and techniques that identify and mitigate emerging risks to privacy. The purpose of this strategy is to help society realize the benefits of information technologies while minimizing their negative societal impact. Strategies for minimizing potential risks to privacy must consider a range of opportunities, from minimizing data collections to proper safeguarding of data once collected to controlling how data is used.

To achieve this objective, the NPRS calls for research along a continuum of challenges, from how people understand privacy in different situations and how their privacy needs can be formally specified, to how these needs can be respected and how mitigation and remediation can be accomplished should privacy expectations and interests be violated. Finally, the NPRS highlights the need to transition research results to governmental and commercial stakeholders so that they can improve practice as necessary and appropriate. Appendix A summarizes the main steps in the development of the strategy.

2.2 Privacy Characterization

Privacy is surprisingly hard to characterize. A full treatment of privacy requires a consideration of ethics and philosophy, sociology and psychology, law and government, economics, and technology. Embodying such broad considerations, the Federal Government's approach has been guided by the Fair Information Practice Principles (FIPPs), a framework for understanding stakeholder considerations utilizing concepts of fairness, due process, and information security. The Administration's 2012 Consumer Privacy Bill of Rights is based on the FIPPs, supplemented importantly by the concept of "respect for context."[10]

---

[8] "Big Data and Privacy: A Technological Perspective," PCAST, May 2014, http://www.whitehouse.gov/sites/default/files/microsites/ostp/PCAST/pcast_big_data_and_privacy_-_may_2014.pdf.

[9] The White House Office of Science and Technology Policy.

[10] "Consumer Data Privacy in a Networked World: A Framework for Protecting Privacy and Promoting Innovation in the Global Digital Economy," The White House, February 2012, https://www.whitehouse.gov/sites/default/files/privacy-final.pdf.

Research is needed to help bridge the gap between statements of principles and effective implementation in information systems. The Administration's 2014 report on big data[11] provides that privacy "addresses a range of concerns reflecting different types of intrusion into a person's sense of self, each requiring different protections." Privacy can be defined in multiple ways, depending on whether one highlights aspects such as solitude, confidentiality, the control of dissemination of personal information, the control of one's identity, or the negotiation of boundaries of personal spaces. Indeed, privacy definitions and characterizations continue to evolve and are an open research question. Privacy R&D should not be limited by any particular view or definition of privacy and should be explored from many perspectives. Research examining the usefulness of different approaches and their applicability to general or specific privacy challenges should accompany such explorations.

The research of the strategy outlined in this document is based on a privacy characterization that is a combination of four key concepts: *subjects*, *data*, *actions*, and *context*, as depicted in Figure 1.

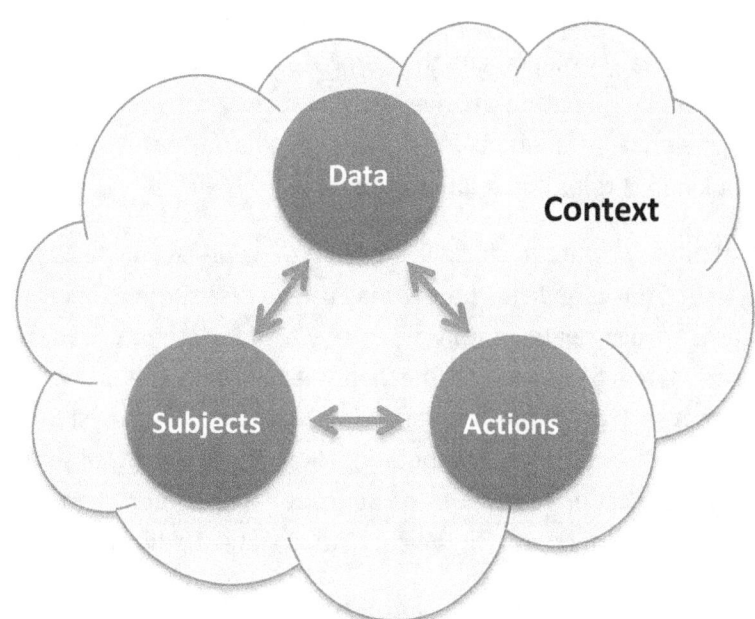

Figure 1: NPRS privacy characterization.

As a coarse characterization, *subjects* encompasses an individual or a group of individuals, the identity (as well as pseudonymity and anonymity) of individuals and groups and their rights, autonomy, and privacy desires. *Data* encompasses the data and derived information about these individuals and groups. *Actions* encompasses the various data collection, processing, analysis, and retention practices, controls that constrain such practices, as well as impacts (negative and positive) of the collection and use of data on individuals, groups, and society. The interactions among *subjects, data, and actions* and

---

[11] "Big Data: Seizing Opportunities, Preserving Values," The White House, May 2014, http://www.whitehouse.gov/sites/default/files/docs/big_data_privacy_report_may_1_2014.pdf.

the interpretation of those interactions and the risk of harm are influenced and conditioned by the *context* in which they interact.

Within this characterization, "privacy" concerns the proper and responsible collection, creation, use, processing, sharing, transfer, disclosure, storage, security, retention, and disposal of information about people. This includes decisions by entities about when *not* to collect, *not* to create, *not* to transfer and *not* to permit certain uses of information to protect legitimate privacy interests.

2.3 Key Challenges for Privacy

The following challenges motivate the research priorities for this strategy.

2.3.1 Influence of Context on Privacy

Individuals share personal data with people or organizations within a particular community for specific purposes. For example, individuals may share their medical status with health care professionals, product preferences with retailers, legal interests with law firms, spiritual concerns with religious organizations, and trip plans with travel agents. The community provides a context for sharing data. When information shared with one community shows up in another outside of the intended context, people may feel a sense of privacy violation and the purposes and values of those contexts might be undermined as well. The contextual nature of privacy makes it clear that questions about privacy necessarily imply specifying privacy for whom and against what harm, the content, the motivation, the conditions, and for what kinds of roles and relationships.

The contextual nature of privacy creates a challenge for designing privacy-protecting systems because people will consider privacy from varied viewpoints, may use diverse terminologies to express their privacy concerns, perceive privacy-related harms differently, and vary their privacy requirements with circumstances. Moreover, system designers lack mechanisms to specify the properties that comprise privacy and to establish that such properties are satisfied by some deployed system. Existing techniques for specifying IT systems and the underlying computational models are not well suited for privacy. For example, existing system specification techniques do not capture "intended purpose" or "expected use;" however, such characterizations are crucial for the contextual view of privacy.

2.3.2 Transparency in Data Collection, Use, and Retention

Providing transparency about data collection and use practices has proven difficult. The traditional notice and choice framework, in which data collectors/users set forth practices in lengthy privacy policies and deem individuals to have read, understood, and consented to them, has its limits. Privacy notices that are sufficiently detailed become too long for individuals to read and give meaningful consent, while notices that are phrased broadly in order to cover all anticipated future uses lack sufficient details for consent to be meaningful. Today, there are so many organizations seeking to collect and use information that individuals realistically do not have the ability to evaluate each collection notice and associated data use. Looking forward, as surroundings are increasingly instrumented with sensors that continuously collect data in domains such as transportation, environmental control, or public safety, protecting privacy through existing disclosure mechanisms may be even more challenging.

Better solutions are needed to support the various purposes of transparency, for consent and choice for individuals and for oversight by regulators.

There is also very little public understanding of data retention practices and their potential implications. For instance, the availability and persistence of collected data can belie people's expectations that minute details of their past will not be forever available. It can also contradict individuals' expectations about how collected data will be used, because providing notice of prospective changes in data-handling practices can be challenging. Data longevity also makes it difficult for individuals to withdraw or change their consent regarding particular data uses.

2.3.3 <u>Data Aggregation, Analysis, and Release</u>

Increased capabilities in data collection, aggregation, analysis, and machine learning are fueling the discovery of new patterns, correlations, and knowledge about the world, and an increasing use of classifying and predictive algorithms. Individuals are often unaware of the outcomes of these algorithms and technologies that score and evaluate them for a variety of purposes. Organizations are increasingly relying on non-public algorithms to make a variety of decisions or direct action. However, there is a risk that predictive algorithms could, for example, enable decisions that result in (perhaps unintended) consequences such as bias and discrimination. Unintended consequences can and do occur, and the actual scale and ramifications of them are not known.

The growing interest in publishing statistics, analyses, and raw data held by the Federal Government raises privacy concerns as well. Existing approaches for protecting privacy, such as the removal of personally identifiable information (PII), have not been able to address the privacy risks of large-scale data collection, analytics, and release. As more information about individuals is retained and made available, data analytics can often be used to link sensitive information back to individuals, despite efforts to anonymize data. This situation creates opportunities for personal information to be misused. Other approaches to privacy protection, such as k-anonymity[12] and differential privacy,[13] can better address some privacy risks while allowing for some beneficial data uses; however, they unavoidably come at a cost in the utility of data.

2.4 Desired Outcome

The goal of this NPRS is to produce knowledge and technology that will enable individuals, commercial entities, and the government to benefit from technological advancements and data use while proactively identifying and mitigating privacy risks. Solutions are needed that will allow people to

---

[12] k-anonymity is a formal model for privacy protection. A dataset provides k-anonymity protection if the information for each person contained in the dataset cannot be distinguished from at least k-1 individuals whose information also appears in the dataset. By L. Sweeney, "k-anonymity: a model for protecting privacy," *International Journal on Uncertainty, Fuzziness and Knowledge-based Systems*, October 2002, pgs. 557-570.

[13] Differential privacy is a formal model for privacy in statistical databases. The model allows one to learn properties of the population as a whole, while protecting the privacy of the individuals in the sample. This is achieved by adding a certain amount of synthetic, "noisy" data to the database such that the contribution of any individual to the overall, statistical properties of the information in the database can't be distinguished. By C. Dwork, Microsoft Research, http://research.microsoft.com/pubs/64346/dwork.pdf.

negotiate and establish boundaries of personal spaces with the world around them, with confidence in the process and in the outcomes of the negotiations.

Privacy creates opportunities for political expression and choice. Privacy protections also provide a space for negotiation between consumers and businesses about data practices. When privacy is not protected, individuals and society suffer from harms, such as erosion of freedom, discrimination, loss of trust in institutions, or reduced innovation from self-censoring by the population.

Sustaining privacy requires technologies targeted for particular use, as well as foundational science and engineering to develop capabilities to analyze contexts that might lead to privacy harms and produce technologies to prevent or mitigate them. Whereas much work to date on privacy has focused on specific narrow technologies and applications, this strategy seeks the development of scientific foundations for privacy that would enable rigorous analysis of the drawbacks, risks, harms, and potential benefits to privacy and society from data collection, processing, and analysis systems; and development of technologies that better protect privacy and allow more robust and precise negotiation of privacy expectations.

This strategy does not attempt to set privacy standards or norms; however, the research outcomes of this strategy should support individuals and the Federal Government in achieving privacy protections and in sustaining societal values as discussed in policy documents including *Cyberspace Policy Review*,[14] *U.S. International Strategy for Cyberspace*,[15] *Consumer Data Privacy in a Networked World*,[16] and *Big Data: Seizing Opportunities, Preserving Values*.[17] Likewise, this strategy does not address privacy policy issues associated with law enforcement or national security (although the research under this strategy should help clarify many related issues). Appendix B further discusses the legal and policy context for privacy in the United States.

Moreover, this strategy does not address how to rectify poor computer security or information protection practices—which can cause privacy harms. Federal research strategy for improving computer and cyber security is presented in the 2016 Federal cybersecurity R&D strategic plan.[18]

---

[14] "Cyberspace Policy Review: Assuring a Trusted and Resilient Information and Communications Infrastructure," The White House, May 2009,
https://www.whitehouse.gov/assets/documents/Cyberspace_Policy_Review_final.pdf.
[15] "U.S. International Strategy for Cyberspace: Prosperity, Security, and Openness in a Networked World," The White House, May 2011,
https://www.whitehouse.gov/sites/default/files/rss_viewer/international_strategy_for_cyberspace.pdf.
[16] "Consumer Data Privacy in a Networked World: a Framework for Protecting Privacy and Promoting Innovation in the Global Digital Economy," The White House, February 2012,
https://www.whitehouse.gov/sites/default/files/privacy-final.pdf.
[17] "Big Data: Seizing Opportunities, Preserving Values," The White House, May 2014,
http://www.whitehouse.gov/sites/default/files/docs/big_data_privacy_report_may_1_2014.pdf.
[18] "Federal Cybersecurity Research and Development Strategic Plan: Ensuring Prosperity and National Security," National Science and Technology Council, February 2016,

Finally, this strategy does not define specific research agendas for individual Federal agencies; rather, it sets objectives for the Executive Branch, within which agencies may pursue priorities consistent with their missions, capabilities, and budgets, so that the overall research portfolio is consistent with this strategy. The priorities will be coordinated within the NITRD Program by facilitating mutual awareness of each agency's strategies and goals, while providing agencies with flexibility to determine responsive research agendas and activities.

3. National Privacy Research Priorities

The following research priorities, jointly established by the information technology research-funding agencies, focus on critical capability gaps in the privacy domain. The priorities provide a strategy; Federal agencies will be responsible for making tactical decisions about how to structure, fund, and execute specific research programs based on their missions and capabilities, so that the overall research portfolio is consistent with this strategy. This strategy is intended to inspire a range of parallel efforts in the private sector.

3.1 Foster multidisciplinary approach to privacy research and solutions

This strategy aims to advance research that will improve government agencies' ability to protect privacy while executing their missions and responsibilities, and more generally, improve civil society's ability to create systems that collect and process information in a manner that respects privacy, ensures fairness, and prevents unfair discrimination. To achieve these objectives, this strategy calls for multidisciplinary research involving disciplines such as computer science, social and behavioral sciences, biomedical science, psychology, economics, law and policy research, and ethics. Multidisciplinary approaches are necessary in order to be able to characterize privacy goals and harms, understand privacy events (acts and actions with the potential to compromise privacy; privacy events may or may not be considered privacy violations and may or may not result in privacy harms), engineer privacy-protecting systems, and recover from privacy violations.

Furthermore, there can be profound challenges to deploying and otherwise maximizing the results of privacy research. Deploying new privacy-aware approaches may require changes in existing technology systems, in business processes, in regulations, and in laws. These costs must be explicitly recognized and addressed; otherwise, many long-term benefits of increased privacy protection will not be realized. Multidisciplinary approaches are needed to understand how the adoption of privacy protections is advanced or impeded by policy and regulatory factors, organizational and business aspects, market competition, and economic and social incentives or disincentives. Multidisciplinary research is needed to

---

https://www.whitehouse.gov/sites/whitehouse.gov/files/documents/2016_Federal_Cybersecurity_Research_and_Development_Stratgeic_Plan.pdf.

gain insight into whether and when privacy protections are addressed best technologically or through ethics and policy, or some combination of all methods.

Efforts to maximize adoption of privacy protections must also consider potential market inefficiencies, such as asymmetric information between consumers and producers, where there is an aspect of product quality which consumers have much less ability to evaluate compared to producers. This may lead to underinvestment in producing that aspect of quality—in this case, in producing privacy-protective features. Learning from fields with similar potential market inefficiencies (e.g. product safety, environmental pollution) may provide some research models for types and combination of solutions to address and support adoption of privacy protections.

3.2 Understand and measure privacy desires and impacts

Privacy desires are often diverse, context specific, dynamic, difficult to predict, and difficult to measure. Research is needed to develop methods and technologies that provide the capabilities to characterize the various and evolving desires, expectations, norms and rules for activities, information disclosure, and data flows in the digital realm that involve private information. Effective techniques to understand privacy desires in context and over time will strengthen the development of techniques that assist individuals in making and controlling their privacy choices, in anticipating potential privacy issues with introduction of new technologies, and in capturing privacy requirements for the purposes of building privacy-protecting systems. Research is also needed to understand the overall benefits of privacy for society and the ways privacy interacts with other societal goals.

System designers and developers need to better understand what people value regarding privacy, what are people's privacy desires and expectations, and in what ways privacy might be infringed upon, in order to develop systems that are more respectful of peoples' privacy choices. A better understanding of individuals' privacy interests is also important to understanding what types of information must be given to individuals to enable them to make informed choices about their activities. Furthermore, greater awareness of privacy desires and perceived deviations from those desires can inform social and legal policy.

However, achieving such understanding is difficult. Privacy desires can vary by generation, cultural subgroup, national interest, socioeconomic status, and other factors. These variations can make it difficult to draw general conclusions about current privacy norms or predict how these norms may develop over time. Similarly, privacy impacts are shaped by and evolve with the use of new technologies and in new contexts.

Current methods for determining public opinion and gauging privacy desires have significant limitations. Self-reporting assessments, such as surveys, can pose a "privacy paradox" where people profess that they are concerned about privacy, but their on-line actions seem not to be driven by those concerns. Newer techniques for surveying public opinion—for example, by analyzing social media—are promising, but these techniques can be systematically biased, miss important population segments, or be manipulated. Alternatively, behavioral assessments and measurements (analyzing peoples' actual behavior and choices as opposed to their self-assessments) are also problematic, as it is difficult to tease out peoples' privacy desires from actions that they perform within the constraints of a particular IT environment. The IT environment within which the behavior takes place guides individuals' behavior and the behavior itself may not be a good indicator of the actual privacy desires.

In addition to measuring privacy desires, it is important to be able to measure privacy impacts and compare them with privacy desires. Some privacy impacts may occur as the result of a specific event (for example, a data breach) or the introduction of a new process or technology that helps to protect privacy or increases privacy risk. Other impacts may occur as the result of an accumulation of disparate data over time that, when combined, reveal private information or result in inferences not possible in isolation. It is necessary to systematically identify and assess privacy impacts and desires, and consider how they interact with other goals of individuals, organizations, and society as a whole such as convenience, cost savings, and utility for public health and safety.

Various privacy events occur when there are deviations from privacy rules, norms, desires, or expectations of a group or individuals. Research is needed to develop methods and technologies for better understanding, detecting, and assessing such deviations and privacy harms that may occur as a consequence. In particular, solutions are needed to detect privacy events when these events are not directly identifiable by individuals. This can occur, for example, when an algorithm uses inappropriate information for making a decision. Research addressing privacy events should also aim to clarify the wide range of effects of technology on individuals and society, including the chilling effects of data collections.

For these reasons, this strategy calls for research on techniques for understanding and measuring privacy desires and impacts. Such research should include techniques for assessing the emergence, codification, and revision of societal practices, attitudes, and beliefs regarding privacy and harms from privacy events. Addressing these issues must involve technological, behavioral, economic, cultural, social, educational, psychological, ethical, and historical perspectives and related analyses.

Explicit in the improved understanding of privacy desires and impacts must also be the ability to define various privacy objectives (e.g., individual control, accountability, respect for context, and transparency) and the ability to measure how information systems meet or don't meet those objectives. The measurements should aid individuals in helping them make informed privacy-related decisions as well as support machine-based analysis and reasoning.

Key research questions include:

- What research methods most reliably and validly sample, measure, and represent people's privacy desires, expectations, attitudes, beliefs, and interests in one or more communities?
- To what extent do privacy desires, expectations, attitudes, beliefs, and interests vary by generation, by cultural subgroup, by national interest, by socioeconomic status, or by other demarcations?

- How and why do privacy desires, expectations, attitudes, beliefs, and interests change? Among groups or subgroups, do certain factors influence the emergence of privacy expectations and beliefs regarding privacy more than others, and if so, why?
- What incentives can effectively promote privacy and the adoption of privacy-enhancing technologies, policies, and practices?
- What impacts have privacy incentives had on the full range of social values such as social justice, economic growth and security, and innovation?
- To what extent do incentives, such as sharing personal data for access to "free" services, modulate privacy expectations, attitudes, beliefs, and interests?
- What methods and technologies could identify privacy events and other privacy impacts effectively and efficiently? What methods would be effective for disclosing this information to affected parties and systems?
- How do privacy events become regarded as privacy harms by individuals or groups? How can privacy harms be recognized, measured, and assessed?
- How do privacy events affect peoples' behavior? How can the "chilling effects" of privacy events be measured?
- What information and methods can effectively inform and enable decisions regarding people's privacy desires in the policy, regulatory, and legislative domains?
- To what extent does the public understand how technological and economic factors affect their privacy, and to what extent do people understand power and information asymmetries between individuals and data collectors/users?
- How do different privacy desires, expectations, attitudes, beliefs, and interests in other countries (if they exist) drive any differences in privacy laws and regulations?
- What kinds of formalisms could define privacy objectives and impacts, and what techniques and metrics could be used to measure how information processing systems meet those objectives?
- How can the relationship of privacy objectives and other objectives of individuals, organizations, and society be understood and assessed?
- How can the effects of privacy policy approaches on privacy incidents and markets, both domestically and internationally, be evaluated?

3.3 Develop system design methods to incorporate privacy desires, requirements, and controls

Systems engineering is an interdisciplinary approach to organizing the total technical and managerial effort required to transform a set of stakeholder needs, expectations, and constraints into a solution and to support that solution throughout its life. When systems process personal information, whether by collecting, analyzing, generating, disclosing, retaining, or otherwise using the information, they can impact privacy of individuals. System designers need to account for individuals as stakeholders in the overall development of the solution. However, designing for privacy does not today have parity with other disciplines when it comes to engineering solutions that capture the appropriate protections and stakeholder interests for privacy. Designing for privacy must connect individuals' privacy desires with system requirements and controls in a way that effectively bridges the aspirations with development.

System designers often lack appropriate tools for designing systems that incorporate effective privacy requirements and controls. Even when designers do consider privacy at the beginning of the design process, they lack a systematic approach for understanding and assessing the risks that a system might pose to privacy, for identifying and expressing privacy requirements for a system, and for designing controls that can achieve those goals. In contrast to other fields, privacy lacks models that provide quantifiable methods for describing risk.

Risk identification and management is only one part of overall systems engineering. System engineers also need consistent privacy objectives oriented around engineering processes to allow them to develop system-level requirements and capabilities to implement privacy policies. System owners are often faced with conflicts among various organizational objectives such as efficiency, cost, functionality, mission, and system quality attributes (e.g., security, safety, privacy, etc.) that force them to make tradeoffs. Without privacy engineering objectives, it is more difficult for system owners and engineers to analyze how privacy interacts with other system objectives. Research is needed to find approaches that will minimize such tradeoffs and allow engineers to identify solutions that maximize both privacy and other objectives to the greatest extent possible.

Furthermore, research should be aimed at developing tools to help system designers choose, test, and validate among different privacy controls, as well as developing approaches for combining multiple privacy-preserving mechanisms in operational systems. For example, as a tool for bridging the gap between privacy principles and system implementation, design patterns could enable system designers to better apply and share solutions to common privacy problems.

With better frameworks and tools for privacy engineering and risk management, research can advance around technical controls and how system designers can most effectively apply them in systems. Some privacy controls can be categorized as organizational controls, but there are many cryptography-based technologies that could be deployed at the system level to achieve privacy-positive outcomes. Making combined progress on frameworks, risk models, and technical controls will improve the capability to assess privacy risk in specific systems and compare the effectiveness of different privacy controls. Ultimately these techniques should make it possible to transform measurements into end-to-end determinations as to how processing of personal information affects privacy.

Research is needed to develop methodologies to connect evolving privacy desires to system design and to development. In security, the threats may change but security objectives and design and engineering methods are quite stable and use risk-based processes to account for changing threat environments. Likewise, it is important to define consistent privacy-related objectives and processes that allow for the interchange between privacy desires and the evolving technology environment.

Key research questions include:

- How can privacy risk be modeled to support privacy risk identification and management?
- What kinds of system properties can be associated with privacy to support the implementation of privacy principles and policies?
- How should privacy properties be characterized, and how can they be assessed or quantified?
- What privacy design patterns and use cases describe common solutions that would assist system designers, particularly in emerging areas such as smart cyber-physical systems and the Internet of Things?
- How can privacy-enhancing cryptographic technologies be developed to scale, as well as be integrated into the functional requirements and standards that are already widely adopted in systems?
- What metrics can be used to assess the effectiveness of privacy controls?
- How can privacy risk be considered and controlled in concert with system and data utility needs?
- What metrics and measurements can measure both privacy and system utility, to understand the tradeoffs between the two, and to support the development of systems that can maximize both?

3.4 Increase transparency of data collection, sharing, use, and retention

Individuals face considerable burdens in understanding today's complex and dynamic information ecosystem. While some information is collected from individuals in a relatively transparent fashion, a great deal of information may be collected without an individual's knowledge and by data collectors with whom the individual has no relationship. The growing use of sensors in both the home and in public space for public safety, transportation, and environmental purposes has also resulted in the collection of vast amounts of data on individuals. Because much of this data collection and use is invisible to individuals, they often are unaware of when data about them is collected or for what purposes it will be used. In addition, individuals often do not understand the extent to which data about them is shared with third parties. This lack of awareness leads to the individual being unable to make informed decisions about the tradeoffs involved in sharing personal information in exchange for some personal or social benefit.

Research designed to increase transparency of data collection and use would enable individuals to better evaluate the privacy implications and potential benefits of their activities and would permit data collectors/users to develop data practices that respect and protect individuals' privacy desires. Increased transparency of data collection and use will also enable privacy technologists to develop solutions that better address the needs of individuals and data collectors/users, and it will provide regulators with improved visibility into data collection and use activities.

The notice-and-choice approach has attempted to promote transparency for otherwise invisible practices. Today, many data collectors disclose their data practices through privacy policies. Public posting of privacy policies promotes data collectors' accountability for their practices; however, privacy policies are often difficult to locate, overloaded with jargon, and ambiguous or open-ended in their meaning, rendering them confusing and even incomprehensible. The burden on individuals to read and understand these policies is further compounded in the mobile context where, because of the small size of the device, a privacy policy may be spread out over 100 separate screens. Some data collectors/users have begun to experiment with innovative approaches such as "just-in-time" disclosure that provides small, understandable amounts of information at relevant points in a transaction. The Administration facilitated a multistakeholder effort to standardize the presentation of privacy policies for mobile apps to enhance their legibility, accessibility, and ubiquity.[19] However, more research is needed to determine how traditional and newer transparency mechanisms can be improved and to identify other promising methods of disclosure.

Data have also become very durable. Because electronic storage is inexpensive and takes up very little space, data collectors are not only collecting greater amounts of information than they have in the past, they are also storing that information for longer periods. Accordingly, developing effective means for informing individuals about prospective uses of their information is critical in achieving information symmetry between people and data collectors/users.

In addition, there has been insufficient effort to develop means to increase consumer awareness and understanding of today's systems, business practices, and information flows. Greater understanding regarding specific business models, the tools available to individuals to control the collection and use of their data, and the benefits and privacy implications of various data uses would alleviate much of the existing information disparity between people and data collectors/users.

Key research questions include:

- What type(s) of experimental studies and field trials should be used to discover information asymmetry?
- Can tools or automated systems be built to measure and report information flows? Is it possible to measure such flows without inherently producing more privacy risk?
- What techniques could be effective in informing individuals about the information practices of data collectors/users, and in informing data collectors/users about the desires and privacy preferences of individuals?
- How can the format and lexicon for describing data practices across industries be standardized, taking into account the inevitability of changes in technology over time? What other measures could improve individuals' ability to compare data practices across the range of data collectors/users, thereby encouraging competition on privacy issues?
- What might be the appropriate level of transparency and choice for prospective changes to data-handling practices? How can the impact of these changes be measured?
- How can individuals be provided with notice about the practices of data collectors that collect and use data without directly interacting with individuals?

---

[19] https://www.ntia.doc.gov/other-publication/2013/privacy-multistakeholder-process-mobile-application-transparency.

- How can notice and choice be standardized and conveyed in ways that facilitate automation and reduce transaction costs for users and stakeholders?
- How can privacy policies be improved to ensure reader comprehension, including examination of the efficacy of disclosure attributes such as text, font, and icons or graphics?
- How can data collectors/users provide meaningful notice of their data practices on mobile and similar devices? How effective are "just-in-time" disclosures?
- In what situations is the traditional notice-and-choice approach ineffective without other types of protections?
- How should the effectiveness of transparency mechanisms be evaluated?

3.5 Assure that information flows and use are consistent with privacy rules

Individuals not only need to understand the rules that govern flows and use of personal data, they need to have confidence that those rules are observed in practice. Research is needed to advance technologies that can assure that personal data are linked with the rules appropriate for the context in which they are collected and that operations applied to those data are governed by those rules.[20] Research is also needed to determine whether privacy rules for the output data could be derived from rules associated with the inputs, the processing, and the permissible use (context) for the outputs. Attaining such capabilities could require new computational models and languages for making precise and implementing as code the essential premises about intent and desires for information use that are implicit when privacy is viewed as contextual.

For example, techniques are needed that allow data to be reliably tagged and processed in a way that preserves the context under which they were collected and are maintained. "Context" is a broad concept that might include a person's consent and preferences, regulatory requirements, geographical location, or data sharing agreements. Such tags could capture the acceptable data uses signaled by the individuals and allow data collectors to ensure that subsequent users will continue to honor both the person's permissions and the specific requirements for individual data. More broadly, these techniques should facilitate people's expression of privacy preferences and their implementation.

Ways to associate rules with code are also needed, so that other code can verify that rules are being faithfully executed and so that the resulting data can be associated with the rules under which they were collected and processed. Together, these approaches can help create *accountable* systems where violations of privacy policy can be detected and made known to affected persons.

Improved technology for managing data use would make it possible for data-processing and storage organizations to determine, rapidly and reliably, if their handling of private information meets legal, regulatory, and ethical standards. Such technology would have the additional benefits of allowing erroneous data to be found and either corrected or deleted.

---

[20] "Big Data and Privacy: A Technological Perspective," PCAST, May 2014, https://www.whitehouse.gov/sites/default/files/microsites/ostp/PCAST/pcast_big_data_and_privacy_-_may_2014.pdf.

These approaches will help ensure that the responsibility for using personal data in accordance with the person's preferences will rest with data collectors, processors, aggregators and service providers. They will also help support social norms and deter inappropriate data actions.

Key research questions include:

- What are usable methods for specifying and managing information-flow based controls?
- How can hardware or software methods for establishing trustworthy execution environments support secure management of information flows and compliance with privacy policies?
- Can methods for tracking, assuring, and archiving the provenance of data and software components be used to assure privacy compliance?
- Can data provenance be implemented in a way that does not itself violate privacy?
- What program analysis methods can be developed for various kinds of information flow properties and privacy policy languages that are meaningful to legal experts, yet have precise semantics that system developers can use to restrict and provide accountability for how their code operates on personal information of users?
- Are there effective methods for understanding the flow of personal data through systems of computer programs?
- In what ways can privacy rules for the results of data processing be derived from privacy rules of the inputs, processing, and context?
- How can the change in value or sensitivity of data, as they are combined with other information, be accounted for and properly acted upon by information processing systems?
- Can access control systems that incorporate usage-based and purpose-based constraints be adapted to the range of privacy issues now faced by system designers?
- Are there effective information disclosure controls, methods for de-identifying data, and means for assessing these de-identification methods?
- Can anonymous and pseudonymous computing, computing with obscured or encrypted data, and management of multiple identities be made efficient and practical?
- Can existing Internet infrastructure and protocols be redesigned to better support privacy (i.e., support anonymous, censorship-resistant, and metadata-hiding communications)? Can privacy be built into core Internet services without adversely affecting cybersecurity?

3.6 Develop approaches for remediation and recovery

Recovering from perceived or actual privacy violations requires remedies. Frequently, there is no legal recourse or even legal recognition that a privacy violation has taken place. Existing recovery mechanisms are limited and are inconsistent in their efficacy. The difficulty of recovery magnifies the importance of privacy risks and increases the impact of the information asymmetry between individuals and data collectors/users. By understanding how data actions operate (collections, flows, uses, disclosures of certain information, etc.) and how they may result in harm, better approaches for recovery might be devised.

Research is needed to measure the efficacy of existing technical, economic, and legal redress mechanisms (e.g., credit freezes and monitoring, privacy-protection insurance, liability regimes for privacy compromises), and to evaluate the consequences of a lack of redress. New approaches for recovering from privacy events need to be developed that are fast, predictable, and easy to implement. For example, research is needed to develop approaches for more quickly recovering from data breaches and problematic releases. Remediation techniques might also provide the capabilities to correct or delete erroneous data about individuals, exclude improperly used data, and effect a change in the processing systems that caused the privacy event. Research is also needed to develop new techniques to effect redress, such as rendering the data useless, as well as mechanisms to delete or "forget" information.

Key research questions include:

- What technological mechanisms would effectively remediate a privacy event?
- How can the effectiveness of remediation and recovery mechanisms be evaluated in terms of their financial, psychological, and societal impact?
- What effect does the existence of remediation and recovery mechanisms have on the likelihood of privacy events?
- What effect does the use of remediation and recovery have on the investment in more robust privacy technologies?
- How could privacy-protecting and privacy-recovery technologies be integrated to create more effective and efficient solutions?

3.7 Reduce privacy risks of analytical algorithms

Algorithms that analyze and predict human behavior and performance, detect fraud, or perform other important functions have been used by government and business for decades. The operation of predictive algorithms can benefit or harm individuals by categorizing a person in ways that enhance or limit his or her options and opportunities.

Increasingly, analytical algorithms are being combined with large-scale data sources, and systems are acting upon the results of the algorithmic determination. "Analytical algorithms" are algorithms for prioritizing, classifying, filtering, and predicting. Their use can create privacy issues when the information used by algorithms is inappropriate or inaccurate, when incorrect decisions occur, when there is no reasonable means of redress, when an individual's autonomy is directly related to algorithmic scoring, or when the use of predictive algorithms chills desirable behavior or encourages other privacy harms.

There are gaps in public knowledge about the range of data-intensive analytical algorithms that are in use, what they are used for, and their susceptibility to error and misuse. It is often unclear if such algorithms have a disparate impact on certain gender, age, racial, or economic groups even when the algorithm does not explicitly use those attributes. Use of such algorithms for employment, housing, policing, and other critical areas potentially implicates Federal equal opportunity laws and demands greater transparency. Indeed, the lack of transparency around companies providing consumer data for credit and other eligibility determinations led to the adoption of the Fair Credit Reporting Act, passed in 1970. However, it is currently difficult, and sometimes infeasible, for those using these algorithms to know if they are producing a disparate impact. Outcome-based studies have identified these issues in the past, but such studies take substantial time and effort, and may not be feasible when an algorithm is re-trained on a weekly or daily basis—as might be done to customize the decisions of an algorithm using current events.

Many anticipated uses of predictive algorithms require that the outcomes of the algorithms be explainable for reasons of accountability, transparency, and auditing. In some cases, it may be appropriate (or legally required) for individuals to be able to control whether certain types of data are used in decision-making. For instance, the Equal Credit Opportunity Act of 1974 prohibits credit discrimination on the basis of race, color, religion, national origin, sex, marital status, age, or because a person receives public assistance. However, many analytical algorithms in use today provide little clarity in these areas.

Research is needed to understand the current and planned usage of these algorithms, as well as to develop methods to increase transparency and improve accountability when these algorithms are employed. Improved capabilities are also needed to understand people's concerns, the type and extent of control that is feasible and how to present information to both application developers and end users as new applications of predictive algorithms arise. Techniques are also needed to detect, correct, and redress errors or harm that these algorithms might cause.

Key research questions include:

- In what ways do analytical algorithms and systems that act upon the results of the algorithms adversely affect individuals or groups of people?
- What types of concerns do individuals have with respect to analytical and predictive algorithms, and what information do they need to address these concerns? How can this information be effectively conveyed to an individual?
- How can the provenance, accuracy, and quality of data used in making a decision or a prediction about an individual or groups be assessed?
- How can the compatibility between datasets and analytical algorithms be assessed?
- What are the impacts on individuals or groups when analytical algorithms use erroneous or inaccurate data?
- How can the decisions or predictions made by analytical algorithms be measured and assessed for compliance with legal requirements?
- How can analytical algorithms be designed to provide increased transparency, accountability, and auditing, and to minimize adverse effects on individuals or groups? What are practicable algorithm discovery and intervention mechanisms for individuals, the government, and industry?

- What are the impacts of analytical algorithms on individuals' autonomy and agency (i.e., the ability to make independent and free choices)? In what ways do analytical algorithms create a structure that determines, affects, or limits decisions by individuals?
- How can new technologies and algorithms, and combinations of technologies and algorithms, provide practical and theoretical privacy-preserving data analysis?

Addressing these questions will require a broad research agenda. In addition to research in machine learning and statistics, this strategy will require human factors research in the interplay between people and algorithms.

4. Executing the National Privacy Research Strategy

This strategy presents privacy research priorities based on a joint assessment by Federal agencies participating in the Federal Networking and Information Technology Research and Development (NITRD) Program. As a strategic plan, this document provides guidance to the Executive Branch, policymakers, researchers, and the public in determining how to direct resources into activities that have the greatest potential to generate the greatest impact. It is each agency's responsibility to incorporate these research priorities into its research plans and programs, drawing on its individual strengths and in the context of its mission.

The execution of the National Privacy Research Strategy vests in the Federal agencies, which develop and execute R&D activities, based on their missions and capabilities. The NITRD Program coordinates Federal research investments in various areas of IT through its interagency working groups. In particular, the NITRD Program will ensure that Federal privacy research is well coordinated by helping agencies understand each other's activities, by supporting agencies in minimizing duplication and gaps, promoting and sharing best practices, maximizing impact, by supporting multi-agency collaboration, and by considering how to align the overall NITRD privacy research portfolio with this strategy.

Privacy research funded under this strategy can have a broad range of effects. Research on current practices in the information ecosystem can inform the public debate on privacy issues and provide useful information to policymakers. Research that creates new privacy theory and models creates intellectual frameworks that can help individuals understand privacy, guide the creation of privacy tools, and serve as the basis for further theoretical development. Work on new privacy-enhancing technologies creates prototypes and products that can be used to help society to realize the benefits of networked information technology without sacrificing personal privacy.

Among the first steps in executing the strategy should be a comprehensive review of literature and studies across sectors to assess existing knowledge relevant to the research priorities defined in this plan. Identifying and connecting the variety of research and applied activities in privacy in the many sectors and domains where such work is conducted would be a valuable contribution of the NPRS.

As part of the national strategy, funding agencies are strongly encouraged to create opportunities for researchers to meet with potential users of the research and the public throughout the research process to ensure that research remains aligned with real-world needs and requirements. These opportunities can include "matchmaking" events for researchers to discuss their work, and for potential users to discuss their needs and requirements, ensuring ongoing relationships between researchers, potential customers, and the public, creating opportunities for testing prototypes on real data, and providing governmental assistance for pilot studies and field-testing. Funders should encourage those submitting proposals to have clear plans for technology transfer at the successful conclusion of a research project.

Funding agencies should also explicitly account for the multidisciplinary nature of privacy and enable research that requires joint contributions from two or more disciplines.

While many privacy-preserving techniques and solutions are developed for a specific application, they can frequently be applied in other areas or generalized to broader classes of problems. NITRD agencies are therefore strongly encouraged to create or support the creation of catalogs, or other sharing mechanisms, of privacy-preserving solutions so that such solutions can be shared among agencies and with the public. To help ensure that new and better methods and tools are adopted, the government may need to create incentives or requirements for adoption.

Appendix A: National Privacy Research Strategy Background

Efforts by the Federal Government to protect privacy of individuals are numerous including, for example, the strict confidentiality provisions of the 1929 Census Act which made a disclosure of private information by an agent of the Census Bureau a felony, punishable with up to 2 years of imprisonment. Likewise, supporting and enabling privacy has been a key policy principle of this Administration. The document *Consumer Data Privacy in a Networked World: a Framework for Protecting Privacy and Promoting Innovation in the Global Digital Economy*[21] articulates the Administration's policy on consumer privacy, and the subsequent discussion draft of a legislative proposal[22] suggests a path forward to address privacy challenges in today's information technology-driven world.

The technological challenges and opportunities in protecting privacy have received increased attention as well. The President's Council of Advisors on Science and Technology (PCAST) 2015,[23] 2013,[24] and 2010[25] reviews of the NITRD Program[26] have identified challenges to personal privacy in the digital era as a significant impairment undermining societal benefits from large-scale deployments of networking and IT systems. Underscoring the impairment of societal benefits, a national survey[27] sponsored by the National Telecommunications and Information Administration (NTIA) revealed that 45% of online households have been deterred from participating in online activities such as conducting financial transactions, buying goods or services, or expressing opinions on controversial issues via the Internet, due to concerns about online privacy and security.

Consequently, PCAST has called upon Federal research agencies to create a multi-agency initiative focused on developing scientific and engineering foundations for protecting privacy, which could then be the basis for new technologies and solutions in this space.

---

[21] "Consumer Data Privacy in a Networked World: a Framework for Protecting Privacy and Promoting Innovation in the Global Digital Economy," The White House, February 2012, http://www.whitehouse.gov/sites/default/files/privacy-final.pdf.

[22] "Administration Discussion Draft: Consumer Privacy Bill of Rights Act," The White House, February 2015, https://www.whitehouse.gov/sites/default/files/omb/legislative/letters/cpbr-act-of-2015-discussion-draft.pdf.

[23] "Report to the President and Congress: Ensuring Leadership in Federally Funded Research and Development in Information Technology," PCAST, August 2015, https://www.whitehouse.gov/sites/default/files/microsites/ostp/PCAST/nitrd_report_aug_2015.pdf.

[24] "Designing a Digital Future: Federally Funded Research and Development in Networking and Information Technology," PCAST, January 2013, http://www.whitehouse.gov/sites/default/files/microsites/ostp/pcast-nitrd2013.pdf.

[25] "Designing a Digital Future: Federally Funded Research and Development Networking and Information Technology," PCAST, December 2010, http://www.whitehouse.gov/sites/default/files/microsites/ostp/pcast-nitrd-report-2010.pdf.

[26] Networking and Information Technology Research and Development (NITRD) Program provides a framework in which many US Government agencies come together to coordinate networking and information technology research and development efforts. More information is available at http://www.nitrd.gov.

[27] "Lack of Trust in Internet Privacy and Security May Deter Economic and Other Online Activities," NTIA, May 13, 2016, https://www.ntia.doc.gov/blog/2016/lack-trust-internet-privacy-and-security-may-deter-economic-and-other-online-activities.

In 2014, the National Coordination Office (NCO) for the NITRD Program surveyed Federal agencies to assess the size and scope of Federally-funded privacy research activities. It identified investments of approximately $80 million/year in R&D activities across a broad spectrum of topics and interests related to privacy. The resulting document, *Report on Privacy Research within NITRD*,[28] provides a summary of the survey. The review showed that there are many innovative research projects within NITRD that are classified by their agencies as relevant to a broad range of privacy challenges. At the same time, the survey demonstrated the need for an interagency research framework that will help maximize research impact and ensure the coordination of R&D investments in this area.

Consequently, NITRD began examining both Governmental and societal needs in privacy-enhancing technologies and began defining a framework for research to guide Federal R&D investments in this area. In September 2014, the NITRD Cyber Security and Information Assurance Research and Development Senior Steering Group (CSIA R&D SSG) convened a task group of representatives from various agencies, including Air Force Office of Scientific Research (AFOSR), Census Bureau, Defense Advanced Research Projects Agency (DARPA), Department of Homeland Security (DHS), Department of Energy (DOE), Federal Bureau of Investigation (FBI), Federal Trade Commission (FTC), Intelligence Advanced Research Projects Activity (IARPA), Office of the Director of National Intelligence (ODNI), Office of Naval Research (ONR), Office of the Secretary of Defense (OSD), Office of Science and Technology Policy (OSTP), National Institute of Standards and Technology (NIST), National Institutes of Health (NIH), National Security Agency (NSA), and the National Science Foundation (NSF). CSIA R&D SSG tasked the group with developing a strategy to establish objectives and prioritization guidance for Federally-funded privacy research, providing a framework for coordinating R&D in privacy-enhancing technologies, and encouraging multi-disciplinary research that recognizes the responsibilities of the Government and the needs of society, as well as enhances opportunities for innovation in the digital realm.

The task group reviewed agency needs and existing research activities related to privacy. The group also obtained public input in three ways: (1) by issuing a Request For Information published in the Federal Register in September 2014, (2) by hosting a National Privacy Research Strategy Workshop in Arlington, Virginia in February 2015, and (3) by reviewing the report *Towards a Privacy Research Roadmap for the Computing Community* prepared by the Computing Community Consortium in May 2015. Details for these engagements are available on the NITRD website.[29]

---

[28] "Report on Privacy Research within NITRD," National Coordination Office for NITRD, April 2014, https://www.nitrd.gov/Pubs/Report_on_Privacy_Research_within_NITRD.pdf.
[29] National Privacy Research Strategy page, NITRD, https://www.nitrd.gov/cybersecurity/NationalPrivacyResearchStrategy.aspx.

Appendix B: Legal and Policy Context for Privacy

The U.S. privacy regulatory structure encompasses three basic areas: regulation of commercial entities, government delivery of services, and national security and law enforcement. Each of these areas has a long history of law and policymaking aimed at protecting individual privacy from intrusions by private and governmental actors. These existing laws and policy approaches have begun the work of developing a conceptual basis for privacy, articulating basic expectations and values, and establishing principles such as use limitation and access.

When considering privacy in the public sector, the Fair Information Practice Principles (FIPPs)[30] have shaped Federal laws, regulations, and guidance. The Privacy Act of 1974 is the foundation for privacy protection at the Federal level, and there are similar statutes among the states. The Privacy Act establishes obligations for Federal agencies to limit information collection and maintain accurate information about systems of records, about conditions for disclosure, about provisions for individuals' access to their information, as well as requirements for how data can be shared among separate systems of records. The Privacy Act is often augmented at the agency level through additional statutes or regulations that specifically protect materials such as tax information, census filings, student information, and other kinds of information and, in the process, reflecting various FIPPs principles such as use limitation, purpose specification, security safeguards, and accountability. "Appendix-J" of NIST Special Publication 800-53, Security and Privacy Controls for Federal Information Systems and Organizations,[31] describes 25 different privacy controls that have been implemented by the Federal Government, providing the agencies with supplemental guidance and the appropriate legislative justification for each one. Based on the FIPPs and reflecting best practices, the privacy control catalog is intended to complement and augment Federal information security programs, and reflects the ever-increasing importance of the intersection of privacy and information security programs.

Regulation of commercial actors has become an area of tremendous importance in the U.S. privacy structure as advances in IT have led to novel uses of personal information across a variety of industries. Whereas the privacy laws of many other nations protect all personal data broadly, the U.S. consumer data protection structure has no comprehensive statutory protection specifically addressing privacy

---

[30] First presented in the "Records, Computers and the Rights of Citizens," Report of the Secretary's Advisory Committee on Automated Personal Data Systems, U.S. Department of Health, Education & Welfare, July 1973, https://www.justice.gov/opcl/docs/rec-com-rights.pdf. The principles were subsequently tailored by policy documents, such as by the "Privacy Policy Guidance Memorandum (2008), Department of Homeland Security, http://www.dhs.gov/xlibrary/assets/privacy/privacy_policyguide_2008-01.pdf, by the "National Strategy for Trusted Identities in Cyberspace: Enhancing Online Choice, Efficiency, Security, and Privacy," The White House, April 2011, https://www.whitehouse.gov/sites/default/files/rss_viewer/NSTICstrategy_041511.pdf, and by the "Consumer Data Privacy in a Networked World: A Framework for Protecting Privacy and Promoting Innovation in the Global Digital Economy," The White House, February 2012, https://www.whitehouse.gov/sites/default/files/privacy-final.pdf.

[31] "Security and Privacy Controls for Federal Information Systems and Organizations," NIST Special Publication 800-53 Revision 4, National Institute of Standards and Technology, April 2013, http://nvlpubs.nist.gov/nistpubs/SpecialPublications/NIST.SP.800-53r4.pdf.

across all sectors. Instead, the U.S. approach is sectoral, with most data privacy statutes only applying to specific sectors such as health care, education, communications, and financial services. The sectoral approach permits controls tailored to particular context, but can also leave gaps. For instance, between 1974 and 2004, the United States passed legislation providing significant privacy protections for consumer information in government databanks (1974),[32] educational records (1974),[33] financial records (1978),[34] cable television records (1984),[35] e-mail (1986),[36] video rental records (1988),[37] unwanted phone calls (1991),[38] driver's license records (1994),[39] healthcare records (1996),[40] telecommunications data (1996),[41] information collected from children online (2001),[42] and satellite television records (2004).[43] In each of these cases, Congress protected information that was collected during the course of obtaining services commonly used by citizens. In addition, the Federal Trade Commission (FTC) can take action against companies engaged in "unfair or deceptive" privacy practices where they, for example, make false or misleading claims about privacy or data security or fail to employ reasonable security measures and, as a result, cause or are likely to cause substantial consumer injury.

In the United States, self-regulation has played an important role in helping to police commercial markets. Self-regulation through trade associations and certification programs can adapt more quickly and in a more tailored fashion than government regulation. Self-regulation is a market-based solution that can quickly reward players who deliver products and policies responsive to consumer needs and desires. In addition, self-regulation can handle a variety of tasks—creating rules, playing a role in enforcement, and/or being involved in adjudication. The notice-and-choice model, based on the right to know about what data is collected and to consent (or withhold consent) from its collection and use, encourages companies to develop privacy policies describing their information collection and use practices so that individuals can make informed choices. Some critics claim, however, that self-regulation, and in particular the notice-and-choice model on which it relies, has failed to provide meaningful protection. Instead of providing transparency and empowering individuals with market choices, critics argue that this model has led to long, incomprehensible privacy policies that individuals do not read and have difficulty understanding and are often substantially more expansive than the actual and expected use of the data. In extreme cases, notice-and-choice has allowed players to engage in aggressive data sharing practices as long as the practices are documented and the consumers give their consent.

---

[32] The Privacy Act of 1974, 5 U.S.C. § 552a.
[33] The Family Educational Rights and Privacy Act (FERPA), 20 U.S.C. § 1232g.
[34] The Right to Financial Privacy Act of 1978, 12 U.S.C. 3401.
[35] The Cable Communications Policy Act of 1984, 47 U.S.C. ch. 5, subch. V–A.
[36] The Electronic Communications Privacy Act of 1986 (ECPA), 18 U.S.C. § 2510-22.
[37] The Video Privacy Protection Act of 1988, 18 U.S.C. § 2710.
[38] The Telephone Consumer Protection Act of 1991 (TCPA), 47 U.S.C. § 227.
[39] The Driver's Privacy Protection Act of 1994, 18 U.S.C. § 2725.
[40] The Health Insurance Portability and Accountability Act of 1996 (HIPAA), Pub.L. 104–191.
[41] The Telecommunications Act of 1996, 47 U.S.C. § 222.
[42] The Children's Online Privacy Protection Act of 1998 (COPPA), 15 U.S.C. § 6501–6506.
[43] Carriage of local television signals by satellite carriers, 47 U.S.C. § 338.

In keeping with its mission of promoting free market competition while preventing "deceptive or unfair practices," the FTC has established itself as a backstop in the self-regulatory scheme. If a company deceives consumers about its compliance with a self-regulatory scheme, the FTC can take action alleging a deceptive practice under the FTC Act. State attorneys general have similar consumer protection authorities and play an important role in collaboration with the FTC.

In 2012, the Administration released a white paper entitled *Consumer Data Privacy in a Networked World: A Framework for Protecting Privacy and Promoting Innovation in the Global Digital Economy.*[44] This paper described a four-point strategy for protecting consumer privacy: the creation of a Consumer Privacy Bill of Rights (CPBR); fostering multistakeholder processes to develop enforceable codes of conduct; strengthening FTC enforcement; and improving global interoperability. The CPBR laid out general principles, including respect for context and individual control, among others, that afforded companies discretion in how they were implemented. The Administration recommended legislation to codify the CBPR and implement a process for the creation of codes of conduct through voluntary participation in multistakeholder processes. The proposed legislation would set forth a process through which the FTC could grant safe harbor status to these codes. Finally, the white paper laid out the goals of increasing global interoperability of privacy enforcement. This framework was put forward in actionable form in 2015 in the Administration's Consumer Privacy Bill of Rights Act Discussion Draft.[45] While this draft was not taken up by Congress, the Administration continues in its belief that it presents the best way forward to both protect consumer privacy and trust while maintaining the flexibility needed to promote innovation and growth.

The third area that has been a significant focus of privacy law and policymaking in the United States is law enforcement and national security. Today, law enforcement and intelligence agencies have the ability to collect, connect, and analyze a wide array of data to create a "virtual picture" of individuals to help with solving crimes, preventing attacks, and tracking terrorists.

Recognizing the privacy concerns that such activities can raise, these activities are bound by the rule of law as well. The legal constraints include Constitutional protections such as First Amendment protection for freedom of speech and Fourth Amendment prohibition on unreasonable searches and seizures. In addition, law enforcement and intelligence agencies are also bound by laws such as the Electronic Communications Privacy Act (ECPA), the Privacy Act, and the Foreign Intelligence Surveillance Act (FISA).

Establishing an effective approach to privacy protection that allows individuals to realize the benefits of information technology without compromising their privacy has been difficult—in part, because of differences in individuals' understanding, attitudes, expectations, and behavior, as well as the rapid pace of change in technology. By focusing research efforts on these challenges and prioritizing the translation

---

[44] "Consumer Data Privacy in a Networked World: A Framework for Protecting Privacy and Promoting Innovation in the Global Digital Economy," The White House, February 2012, https://www.whitehouse.gov/sites/default/files/privacy-final.pdf.

[45] "Administration Discussion Draft: Consumer Privacy Bill of Rights Act," The White House, February 2015, https://www.whitehouse.gov/sites/default/files/omb/legislative/letters/cpbr-act-of-2015-discussion-draft.pdf.

of research results into government policy and commercial imperatives, the NPRS aims to meet and overcome the challenges that have confronted policy- and lawmaking on privacy issues to date.